Department of Defense Implementation of the Federal Data Center Consolidation Initiative: Implications for Federal Information Technology Reform Management

Patricia Moloney Figliola, Coordinator
Specialist in Internet and Telecommunications Policy

Anthony Andrews
Specialist in Energy and Defense Policy

Eric A. Fischer
Senior Specialist in Science and Technology

July 12, 2012

Congressional Research Service

7-5700

www.crs.gov

R42604

CRS Report for Congress ———————————————
Prepared for Members and Committees of Congress

Summary

The Department of Defense (DOD) is the single largest energy consumer in the nation. As the largest owner of federal data centers, with 772, the DOD has more than twice as many centers as any other agency. By consolidating some of its data centers, DOD could have a significant positive impact on energy savings for the federal government. DOD has instituted a number of policy directives, as have all federal agencies, that influence energy use in its data centers.

Data centers are facilities—buildings or parts of buildings—used to store, manage, and disseminate electronic information for a computer network. They house servers, which are computers used to perform network-management functions such as data storage and processing, and communications equipment and devices to connect the servers with the network. Data centers usually draw their power from the electric grid, but they may also contain specialized power conversion and backup equipment to maintain reliable power. Power consumption varies greatly among data centers but is typically many times higher than for other kinds of buildings.

Within the context of the FDCCI, DOD's efforts are intended to address concerns about rising energy demands and costs of data centers, associated increases in carbon emissions, expanding real-estate footprints of data centers, and rising real-estate costs. According to DOD, the Department plans to reduce the number of its data centers by about 30% by 2013, and the number of servers by 25%. DOD intends to use savings generated from consolidation to pay the consolidation costs. DOD also plans to use cloud computing as part of its savings effort.

As with any endeavor being implemented across so many departments and agencies, proper management of the initiative will be crucial to its success and, in turn, to achieving the projected savings. Unlike many programs that are overseen by a single committee, implementation of the FDCCI may require oversight by any committee with legislative jurisdiction over a department or agency. Understanding the management challenges and policy considerations involved with data center consolidation (e.g., balancing up-front costs with ongoing savings, maintaining data security, and maximizing energy savings through facilities design) as well as being aware of the issues specific to implementing the FDCCI are important steps to achieving effective Congressional oversight of the FDCCI. In conducting oversight, Congress may wish to—

1. conduct hearings to monitor the activities of OMB as it manages the FDCCI or the progress of individual departments and agencies as they implement the FDCCI;

2. review FDCCI plans and status reports created internally by the individual department or agency, or externally by GAO or the committee of jurisdiction.

Finally, Congress may wish to examine the current "reach" of the FDCCI and consider whether expanding the initiative to include other agencies, as the GAO has recommended, is appropriate.

Contents

Figures

Tables

Appendixes

Contacts

Introduction

The Department of Defense (DOD) is the single largest energy consumer in the nation, accounting for approximately 63% of the energy consumed by federal buildings/facilities at an annual cost of $3.4 billion (FY2007). A significant component of that energy use entails data storage. As of this date, DOD has twice as many data centers as any other federal agency. By consolidating some of those data centers, DOD could have a significant positive impact on energy savings for the federal government.

Consolidating data centers run by the DOD has been an ongoing effort that began in 1989 with an internal study, *Consolidate ADP Operations and Design Centers in DOD*, and continues today through the Federal Data Center Consolidation Initiative (FDCCI).[1] The FDCCI is intended to reverse the growth in potentially redundant IT infrastructure throughout the federal agencies and mitigate the impact such redundancy has on federal energy consumption.[2]

This report provides the context and background of the FDCCI, using DOD data center consolidation as an example of the government's work in this area. The report provides an overview of data center characteristics, specifically the technology used, power consumption issues, and how data centers are classified. It summarizes how and why the federal government increased its investment in data centers and then later determined that consolidation was a better path forward based on the state of computing and communications technology. The report goes on to describe the historical legislation underlying the current initiative, and concludes with a discussion of possible issues for Congressional oversight or consideration.

General Data Center Characteristics

Data centers are facilities—buildings or parts of buildings—used to store, manage, and disseminate electronic information for a computer network. They house servers, which are computers used to perform network-management functions such as data storage and processing, and communications equipment and devices to connect the servers with the network. These facilities may range in size from small rooms called server closets, or even parts of rooms, within a conventional building, to large dedicated buildings called enterprise-class data centers. Larger centers may be purpose-built or retrofitted.

Data centers usually draw their power from the electric grid, but they may also contain specialized power conversion and backup equipment to maintain reliable power, as well as environmental control equipment to maintain the proper temperature and humidity for the information technology (IT) equipment.

---

[1] The FDCCI Homepage is at http://www.cio.gov/pages.cfm/page/FDCCI.

[2] For example, in 2006, federal servers and data centers consumed an estimated 6 billion kilowatt-hours (kWh) of electricity, an amount which was expected to double by 2011. In addition, in FY2010, about 30% of total federal IT investment was reportedly spent on data center infrastructure, even though agencies used less than 30% of available server capacity on average. Report to Congress on Server and Data Center Energy Efficiency, U.S. Environmental Protection Agency, ENERGY STAR Program, August 2, 2007, p. 7, http://www.energystar.gov/ia/partners/prod_development/downloads/EPA_Datacenter_Report_Congress_Final1.pdf, *EPA Report*.

Users generally access data-center resources via workstations, laptop computers, or other devices running software, such as an Internet browser, that interacts with server software. Many software applications require not just data processing, which drives computing demand, but also large amounts of data storage, which drives the demand for storage equipment in data centers.

Advances in computing technology and related changes in power consumption are the two factors that have driven data center capabilities and trends.

Technology

Over the past several decades, computer processing speeds have increased exponentially while the central processing units (CPU) at the heart of computers have reduced in size. Advanced processing chips have allowed manufacturers to pack more processing into smaller and smaller hardware, allowing a higher ratio of computing power to floor space. This trend, commonly referred to as "increased server rack density," has also led to higher power densities in many data centers. Such increased densities result in increased production of heat, which must be removed to maintain servers within their normal operating ranges. Consequently, cooling the CPU consumes additional power, often more than the CPU consumes itself.

Data center rooms are filled with rows of IT equipment racks that contain servers, storage devices, and network equipment. Data centers include power delivery systems that provide backup power, regulate voltage, and make necessary power conversions. Before reaching the IT equipment rack, electricity is first supplied to an uninterruptible power supply (UPS) unit. The UPS acts as a battery backup to prevent the IT equipment from experiencing power disruptions, which could cause serious business disruption or data loss. In the UPS, the electricity is converted from AC to DC to charge the batteries. Power from the batteries is then reconverted from DC to AC before leaving the UPS. Power leaving the UPS enters a power distribution unit, which sends power directly to the IT equipment in the racks. Electricity consumed in this power delivery chain accounts for a substantial portion of overall building load.

Power Consumption

Power consumption varies greatly among data centers but is typically many times higher than for other kinds of buildings. According to the Federal Energy Management Program (FEMP), a data center can consume as much as 100 times the energy of a typical office building.

Virtually all of the power consumed by a data center results in thermal emissions: Ultimately, a watt of electric power consumed is a watt of heat generated. Data centers use energy to supply three key components: IT equipment, cooling, and power delivery. A significant amount of energy is required just to remove heat (see **Figure 1**). A breakdown of a data center's energy use may show that cooling alone may make up half of its electrical demand, while operating the servers and data storage devices (critical loads) may take up a third or more. Lighting and charging battery-backup UPS make up the balance.

Figure 1. A Typical Data Center Energy Use Pattern

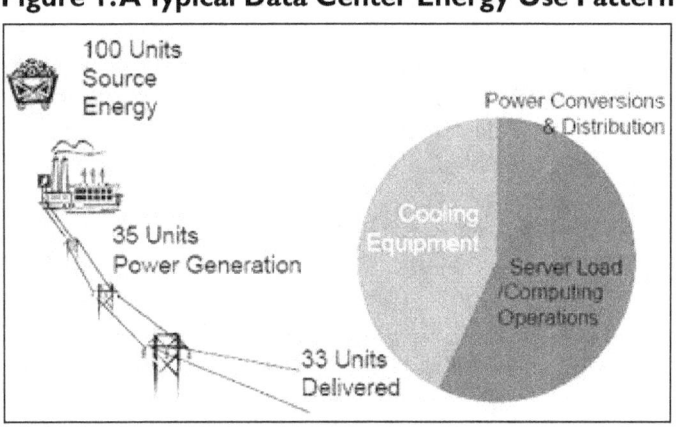

Source: Federal Energy Management Program, "Data Center Energy Consumption Trends," May 30, 2009.

Notes: The figure shows how a data center typically uses energy. Inefficiencies in the generation and transmission of electric power result in only about one-third of the source energy (e.g., from coal or natural gas) being delivered as electricity to the data center. Less than half of that electricity is typically used for computing operations.

Energy-efficient servers are available. The Environmental Protection Agency (EPA) and the Department of Energy (DOE) have developed a specification that servers must meet to receive the Energy Star label. The Federal Acquisition Regulations require agencies to purchase Energy Star products or products designated as energy-efficient under FEMP. In addition, the Institute of Electrical and Electronic Engineers (IEEE), an accredited standards development organization, has begun the process of developing standards for assigning the green "EPEAT"[3] label to qualifying servers. Federal agencies are required to procure EPEAT-registered products for 95% of acquisitions of products for which the label is available.

As server power becomes more concentrated and servers become more energy-efficient, one impact is that, in many cases, power and cooling capacity will be the primary constraints to the expansion of computational capacity within a data center. Server hardware would no longer be the primary cost component of a data center. This represents a significant shift in data center economics that threatens to overwhelm the advances in chip efficiency that have driven the growth of digital information during the past 30 years.

As a result, data center managers must either invest in upgrading the power and cooling infrastructure of existing data centers, or they must build new facilities. Either choice requires significant capital investment and must also include operational changes.

Power Rating vs. Power Demand

Data center managers must also consider hardware's power rating and power demand:

- Power rating is the amount of electrical power that a piece of electronic equipment is designed to draw if it is running at full capacity.

---

[3] "EPEAT" is the Electronic Product Environmental Assessment Tool, an environmental rating system for electronic products designed to help evaluate, compare, and select environmentally preferable products. See http://www.epa.gov/epp/pubs/products/epeat htm.

- Power demand is the amount of power the server actually uses.

Power demand may, in fact, be much lower than the power rating. A server's power consumption will vary depending on the type of server, its power management characteristics, and its use of other IT resources. Estimating a data center's power demand by examining each component's specification sheet yields only the potential maximum power consumption.

In fact, data centers are typically planned to exceed the maximum future estimated power requirements for the expected load. As a result, they are typically oversized, with overall power ratings that exceed true demand requirements—the maximum actual power load drawn by operating servers and cooling equipment—by more than 100% of the required capacity. Such oversizing is often done with the goal of maximizing reliability in the face of expected growth in use.

Throughout the 1990s, servers operated at nearly constant power demands, as the computational load placed on processors and memory caused a negligible variation in overall power consumption. Most servers operate at low computational loads most of the time, and those with power management capability will draw less than their potential power draw. However, the power draw can vary dynamically, such as a power variation of more than 100% between a light-load and a heavy-load draw.

Until recently, data center design and operation has focused on reliability and capacity, with energy efficiency at best a secondary consideration. Some studies indicate that data centers may be using more energy than they need to, even taking reliability needs into account. For example, a 2012 research study conducted by IBM found that one in five data centers was operating at optimum efficiency.[4]

One way to improve data-center energy efficiency is to require users to pay for the energy they actually use. That requires metering. However, for data centers with a wide range of servers, allocating energy costs to users becomes impractical because much of the energy use comes from power equipment, cooling equipment, network devices and other loads not directly associated with a particular user. Furthermore, the cost of metering a particular server and the software required can be extreme. Alternatively, the data center manager can classify servers into a short list of standard types, each with its own energy profile. This would permit allocating total data-center energy across a number of server classes, in order to assign use to individual IT users. Such rationing might be an alternative or a supplement to metering for individual users.

Power Usage Effectiveness (PUE), developed by Green Grid (a global IT consortium) is a metric for data-center energy efficiency that is becoming widely used. PUE is measured by dividing the total electrical power used by a data center by the power used by the IT equipment. Thus, if a data center had a PUE of 2.0, half the power would be consumed by the IT equipment and the other half by other facility components such as cooling, battery back-ups, and so forth. According to EPA, most data centers exhibit a PUE of 1.25 to 3.0.

---

[4] Data Center Operational Efficiency Best Practices, IBM Global Technology Services, p. 3, January 2012, http://public.dhe.ibm.com/common/ssi/ecm/en/rlw03007usen/RLW03007USEN.PDF [Requires sign-up].

The Data Center Trend Arc: From Growth to Consolidation

Worldwide energy use by data centers doubled from 2000 to 2006.[5] During this time, federal agencies built up their data centers independently, leading to a day-to-day surplus of computing power. Because of the energy demands created by this independent growth, the federal government began considering ways to consolidate data centers and find a more cost-effective means of providing sufficient computing power to its agencies while decreasing energy use.

Growth

According to some reports, worldwide energy use by data centers doubled from 2000 to 2006 and a number of factors continue to drive such growth. Among them are electronic financial transactions such as online banking and electronic trading, Internet communication and entertainment, electronic medical records for healthcare, global commerce and services, satellite navigation, and electronic shipment tracking in transportation. Voice-over-Internet protocol[6] communication has also been growing. Increased Internet use is a major factor in the growth in data processing and storage and requires that business and government enterprises host electronic applications in highly reliable data centers with sufficient server capacity to meet peak and growing loads.

Factors contributing to increased use by government include publishing government information and regulations; enhancing disaster recovery, emergency, health and safety services; migrating toward increased "e-government" services (e.g., e-filing of taxes); and access to remote high-speed computing. Government agencies must increase public website hosting to provide online reports and information, and other digital services (e.g., e-filing of taxes, online tracking of items sent through the U.S. Postal Service). In addition, requirements related to homeland security (from e-passports to cybersecurity) and scientific computing in government research institutions add additional IT burdens. State and local governments are also subject to many of the same demands.

In addition to their everyday business-related computer applications, companies are increasingly subject to regulations that require them to collect and store digital records of their business transactions. The most well known regulation is the Sarbanes-Oxley Act, which requires long-term storage of financial records, including electronic records such as email. According to some projections, the number of records that some industries must retain grew at an estimated compound annual growth rate (CAGR) of 50% or greater in the last decade. Business disaster recovery needs are also strong motivators for increasing storage (e.g., duplicate data sets) and establishing redundant data-center equipment and facilities.

---

[5] *EPA Report*, p. 7.

[6] The National Institute of Standards and Technology defines VOIP as the delivery of voice services via packetized data services.

Consolidation

Data center consolidation, both in the private and public sectors, has been an increasing trend for several years (**Figure 2**). The general pattern is consolidation of many smaller data centers into one data center or a few larger ones. Several factors, mostly related to costs, have been cited as contributing to this trend. Among them are the following:

- more efficient use of servers, storage, and staff, including reductions in energy consumed by idle servers;

- reductions in redundancy of hardware, software, and operations requirements, including HVAC;

- increased flexibility in use of servers;

- freed up floor space for other purposes;

- increased reliability of service; and

- improved security.

Figure 2. Data Center Consolidation Trends, 2006 to 2008

Percentages of Surveyed Organizations Citing Specific Actions

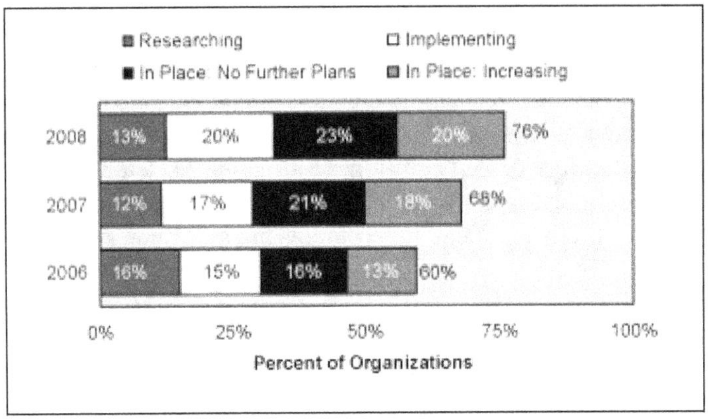

Source: Computer Economics, Inc., "Data Center Consolidation Shows Overwhelmingly Positive ROI," August 2008, http://www.computereconomics.com/article.cfm?id=1386.

Notes: The data are from a survey of more than 200 organizations of various sizes.

Consolidation from a cost-saving perspective may be particularly attractive during times of economic downturn, as it can apparently produce substantial cost savings. For example, for many data centers, under 10% of the servers' capacity is typically used, even though data centers can account for about one-quarter of total IT costs for large enterprises. Annual costs for those facilities are increasing at 10% per year, more than thrice the growth rate of other IT spending.

Given such costs, growth, and inefficiencies, it may seem surprising that more effort has not been made to address them. At least two factors have been cited to explain that pattern. First, the traditional focus of data-center management has primarily been on service and reliability in response to rising demand. This can reduce the priority of efforts to improve energy efficiency

---

and cost savings. Second, organizational fragmentation in the management of data centers—for example, by separating financial from operational responsibilities—and "siloing" of decisions have been cited as significant barriers. As a result, decisions that lead to increased demand may be made with little or no regard to their impacts on data-center energy use and costs.

The goals of the FDCCI largely reflect those factors. (The FDCCI is discussed in detail in the section below, "The Federal Data Center Consolidation Initiative.")

Building Towards the Current Consolidation Initiative

Three documents form the basis of the current consolidation initiative by the federal government.

National Performance Review and OMB Bulletin 96-02, Consolidation of Agency Data Centers

In 1993, the Vice President's National Performance Review recommended that the federal government take advantage of evolving technology to consolidate information-processing services to decrease costs. The Office of Management and Budget (OMB) followed up with Bulletin 96-02—*Consolidation of Agency Data Centers*—which called on federal agencies to consolidate and modernize their data centers, collocate small and mid-tier computer platforms, and outsource small-scale information processing either to other agencies or commercial enterprises.

The Review and OMB bulletin estimated that 30%-50% savings could be obtained in an operational costs report on information infrastructure and "industry experience." While the performance review did include a proposal for an executive order on energy efficiency and water conservation at federal facilities, it made no specific link between energy efficiency and IT. Consolidation of data centers (in the interest of energy-efficiency improvement) appears to be a recent rationale, although energy savings mandates across federal agencies date back several decades.

EPA Report to Congress on Server and Data Center Energy Efficiency

In December 2006, Congress mandated that the EPA study the use of energy efficient computer servers. P.L. 109-431[7] required that the EPA, through the Energy Star program, study and report on the rapid growth and energy consumption of computer data centers by the federal government and private enterprise. The EPA responded with its "Report to Congress on Server and Data Center Energy Efficiency" in August 2007 ("*EPA Report*").[8] This report illustrated the nexus

---

[7] Online at http://www.gpo.gov/fdsys/pkg/PLAW-109publ431/pdf/PLAW-109publ431.pdf.

[8] All information about this report is online at http://www.energystar.gov/index.cfm?c= prod_development.server_efficiency_study.

between data center IT and energy consumption and demonstrated the government's commitment to federal IT reform to support energy conservation and savings.

In the *EPA Report*, published in August 2007, the agency estimated that U.S. data servers had accounted for roughly 1.5% of total U.S. electric consumption in 2006, for approximately 61 billion kWh at a cost of about $4.5 billion. That same year, federal servers and data centers reportedly accounted for approximately 6 billion kWh at a cost of about $450 million—about 10% of that national total use. The *EPA Report* also presented estimates that data-center electricity use in 2006 was more than double than in 2000, and noted that the power and cooling infrastructure supporting that server equipment accounted for 50% of the total consumption.

Projections of Future Data Center Energy Use

The EPA Report developed two five-year projections for data-center energy trends:

- The *current efficiency trends* scenario projected future energy use of U.S. servers and data centers based on observed efficiency trends for IT equipment and site infrastructure systems.

- The *historical trends* scenario did not reflect energy efficiency trends but simply extrapolated observed 2000-2006 energy-use trends into the future. It assumed no future energy-efficiency improvements, and therefore indicated the energy savings already under way.

Under *current efficiency trends,* the report stated that national energy consumption by servers and data centers could nearly double in another five years (i.e., by 2011) to more than 100 billion kWh, representing a $7.4 billion annual electricity cost. The server's and data center's estimated 7-GW peak load on the power grid equaled the output of "about 15 baseload power plants."

The report went on to say that if current trends were to continue, this demand would rise to 12 GW by 2011, "which would require an additional 10 power plants." Those forecasts indicated that unless energy efficiency improved beyond then-current trends, the federal government's electricity cost for servers and data centers could be nearly $740 million annually by 2011, with a peak load of approximately 1.2 GW.

Energy Efficiency

The EPA Report stated that there is significant potential for energy-efficiency improvements in data centers. Although some improvements in energy efficiency were expected if current trends continued, many technologies, either commercially available or soon available, could further improve the energy efficiency of microprocessors, servers, storage devices, network equipment, and infrastructure systems. Other opportunities could accelerate adoption of energy-efficient technologies beyond current trends:

- The *improved operation* scenario included energy-efficiency improvements beyond current trends that are essentially operational in nature and require little or no capital investment. This scenario offered potential electricity savings of more than 20% relative to then-current trends, representing low-cost energy-efficiency opportunities.

- The *best practice* scenario represented the efficiency gains that more widespread adoption of the practices and technologies could obtain using the most energy-efficient facilities in operation. This scenario could reduce electricity use by up to 45% by using available technologies.

- The *state-of-the-art* scenario identified the maximum energy-efficiency savings that available technologies could achieve. This scenario could reduce electricity use by up to 55% compared to then-current efficiency trends, representing the maximum technical potential.

According to the report, those scenarios showed an annual savings potential of about 23 billion-74 billion kWh in 2011 compared to the *current efficiency trends* scenario, reducing the peak load from data centers by the equivalent of up to 15 new power plants and reducing annual electricity costs by $1.6 bilion-$5.1 billion. Based on the assumption that the federal sector accounts for about 10% of electricity use and electricity costs attributable to servers and data centers, the annual savings in federal electricity costs in 2011 could range from $160 million (*improved operation*) to $510 million (*state-of-the-art*). Those gains could be achieved without compromising performance.

Executive Order 13514, Federal Leadership in Environmental, Energy, and Economic Performance

On October 5, 2009, President Obama signed Executive Order 13514, *Federal Leadership in Environmental, Energy, and Economic Performance.*[9] This order directs federal agencies to establish an integrated strategy towards sustainability and makes reductions in greenhouse gas emissions a priority. It also requires federal agencies to increase energy efficiency and "implement best management practices for energy-efficient management of servers and Federal data centers." The order also increases the energy efficiency levels required of new building designs, and sets a target of zero net-energy consumption for new buildings by 2030. It encourages cost-effective, innovative strategies to minimize water and energy consumption—for example, reflective or vegetated roofs. Rehabilitation of federally owned, historic buildings should employ "best practices" and technologies to promote long-term viability. The order also gives priority to the developing site selection procedures to site federal buildings in sustainable locations.

The Federal Data Center Consolidation Initiative

Building on the *EPA Report* and in tandem with Executive Order 13514, as well as in light of the benefits of data center consolidation reported by private sector, in February 2010, the U.S. Chief Information Officer (CIO) announced the FDCCI.[10] The four high-level goals of the initiative are to:[11]

---

[9] Online at http://www.whitehouse.gov/assets/documents/2009fedleader_eo_rel.pdf.

[10] The FDCCI Homepage is at http://www.cio.gov/pages.cfm/page/FDCCI.

[11] Update on the Federal Data Center Consolidation Initiative, Executive Office of the President, October 2010, http://www.cio.gov/documents/State-of-the-Federal-Datacenter-Consolidation-Initiative-Report.pdf.

3. promote the use of "Green IT"[12] by reducing the overall energy and real estate footprint of government data centers;[13]

4. reduce the cost of data center hardware, software, and operations;

5. increase the overall IT security posture of the government; and

6. shift IT investments to more efficient computing platforms and technologies.

The initiative is intended to reverse the growth in potentially redundant IT infrastructure throughout the federal agencies and its significant impact on federal energy consumption.[14]

OMB was charged with executing and managing the initiative and it, in turn, designated two CIOs for each of the 24 participating departments and agencies.[15] OMB required that the agencies submit data center inventories and consolidation plans by the end of August 2010, and provided guidance on key elements to include in the inventories and plans—such as hardware and software assets, goals, schedules, and cost-benefit calculations.

Since the FDCCI was announced, OMB expanded the definition of a data center from facilities over 500 square feet to one that includes data centers of all sizes. This change resulted in an expanded data center baseline of 3,133 centers, an increase from the 2,094 centers originally reported by agencies. In December 2011, the U.S. CIO announced a revised goal of closing over 1,200 of the 3,133 data centers, which was included in the Analytical Perspectives for the President's budget for FY2013.[16] That revision is expected to save $3 billion by 2015.

25-Point Implementation Plan to Reform Federal IT Management

In December 2010, the U.S. CIO released, "A 25-Point Implementation Plan to Reform Federal IT Management."[17] Data center consolidation is the first of the 25 goals outlined: agencies must complete detailed implementation plans for consolidating at least 800 of its 2,100 data centers by 2015—a reduction of almost 40%. By July 2011, 81 data centers had been closed and 373 more were slated for closure by the end of 2012.[18]

---

[12] "Green IT" refers to environmentally sound computing practices that can include a variety of efforts, such as using energy efficient data centers, purchasing computers that meet certain environmental standards, and recycling obsolete electronics.

[13] **Appendix A** contains a summary of laws that compose the federal framework for energy conservation. **Appendix B** contains a summary of Executive Orders that complement the federal framework for energy conservation.

[14] For example, in 2006, federal servers and data centers consumed an estimated 6 billion kilowatt-hours (kWh) of electricity, an amount which was expected to double by 2011. In addition, in FY2010, about 30% of total federal IT investment was reportedly spent on data center infrastructure, even though agencies used less than 30% of available server capacity on average.

[15] The 24 participating departments and agencies are Agriculture, Commerce, Defense, Education, Energy, Health and Human Services, Homeland Security, Housing and Urban Development, Interior, Justice, Labor, State, Transportation, Treasury, Veterans Affairs, Environmental Protection Agency, General Services Administration, National Aeronautics and Space Administration, National Science Foundation, Nuclear Regulatory Commission, Office of Personnel Management, Small Business Administration, Social Security Administration, and U.S. Agency for International Development.

[16] Online at http://www.whitehouse.gov/sites/default/files/omb/budget/fy2013/assets/spec.pdf.

[17] Online at http://www.cio.gov/documents/25-Point-Implementation-Plan-to-Reform-Federal%20IT.pdf.

[18] See http://www.cio.gov/pages.cfm/page/IT-Reform-Task-Force-Will-Drive-Data-Center-Closures. A detailed status report on the progress in closing data centers is available online at https://explore.data.gov/Federal-Government- (continued...)

One related goal is to create a government-wide marketplace for data center availability, aimed at improving use of existing facilities across agencies. Another related goal is shift to a "cloud first" policy[19] across federal agencies. Cloud computing, a rapidly growing means of using computer resources, could reportedly accelerate the consolidation effort, amplify its benefits by reducing duplication of effort and improving efficiency of use, and simplify IT management.

Status of the FDCCI

At the request of Congress, in July 2011, the Government Accountability Office (GAO) published its findings regarding the status of the FDCCI.[20] In its investigation, it found that only one agency (the National Science Foundation) had submitted a complete inventory and no agency had submitted complete plans. However, agency plans still indicated savings of about $700 million through 2015.

In May 2012, GAO provided Congress with a status report on the 25-Point Plan[21] and its work related to implementing the GPRA Modernization Act,[22] which included an update of FDCCI implementation. In those reports, GAO stated that it was continually assessing the updated inventories and plans that departments and agencies had begun posting online in October 2011. As of April 2012, not all agency inventories and plans had been updated to include all required information, such as consolidation milestones, performance metrics, and savings projections.

Department of Defense Data Center Consolidation

DOD accounts for approximately 63% of the energy consumed by federal buildings and other facilities. The department's activities occupy more than 316,000 buildings and an additional 182,000 structures on 536 military installations worldwide. DOD's annual spending on facility energy use was more than $3.4 billion in FY2007. This makes DOD the single largest energy consumer in the nation, even though the agency consumption comprises only 1% of the national total for site-consumed energy.

As the largest owner of federal data centers, with 772 (**Figure 3**), DOD and its military and other constituent services face a complex challenge in implementing the FDCCI. To its benefit in

---

(...continued)

Finances-and-Employment/Federal-Data-Center-Consolidation-Initiative-FDCCI/d5wm-4c37?.

[19] The National Institute for Standards and Technology defines "cloud computing" as "a model for enabling ubiquitous, convenient, on-demand network access to a shared pool of configurable computing resources (e.g., networks, servers, storage, applications, and services) that can be rapidly provisioned and released with minimal management effort or service provider interaction." Additional detail is available online at http://csrc nist.gov/publications/nistpubs/800-145/SP800-145.pdf.

[20] "Data Center Consolidation: Agencies Need to Complete Inventories and Plans to Achieve Expected Savings," GAO-11-565, GAO, July 2011, http://www.gao.gov/products/GAO-11-565. *"Data Center Consolidation."* Another report was published previously, "Opportunities to Reduce Potential Duplication in Government Programs, Save Tax Dollars, and Enhance Revenue," GAO-11-318SP, March 2011, http://www.gao.gov/products/GAO-11-318SP.

[21] "Information Technology Reform: Progress Made; More Needs to Be Done to Complete Actions and Measure Results," GAO-12-745T, GAO, May 24, 2012, http://www.gao.gov/products/GAO-12-745T.

[22] "Managing for Results: GAO's Work Related to the Interim Crosscutting Priority Goals under the GPRA Modernization Act," GAO-12-620R, GAO, May 31, 2012, http://www.gao.gov/products/GAO-12-620R. *"GAO Report, Managing for Results."*

adhering to the schedule for the current initiative, however, DOD has engaged in consolidation efforts over the past few years. In addition, the Secretary of Defense has identified consolidation of IT infrastructure as one of the department's efficiency initiatives announced in August 2010.

DOD has instituted a number of policy directives, as have all federal agencies, that have and will continue to influence energy use in DOD data centers, although most are not targeted specifically to data centers. The FDCCI could lead to a reduction in data-center energy use, at least in the short term. However, in the face of what is likely to be continuously increasing demand for data-center services, gains from consolidation and improved efficiency are expected to plateau, with energy use resuming an upward trajectory subsequently.

Figure 3. Distribution of Federal Data Centers among Agencies, July 2010

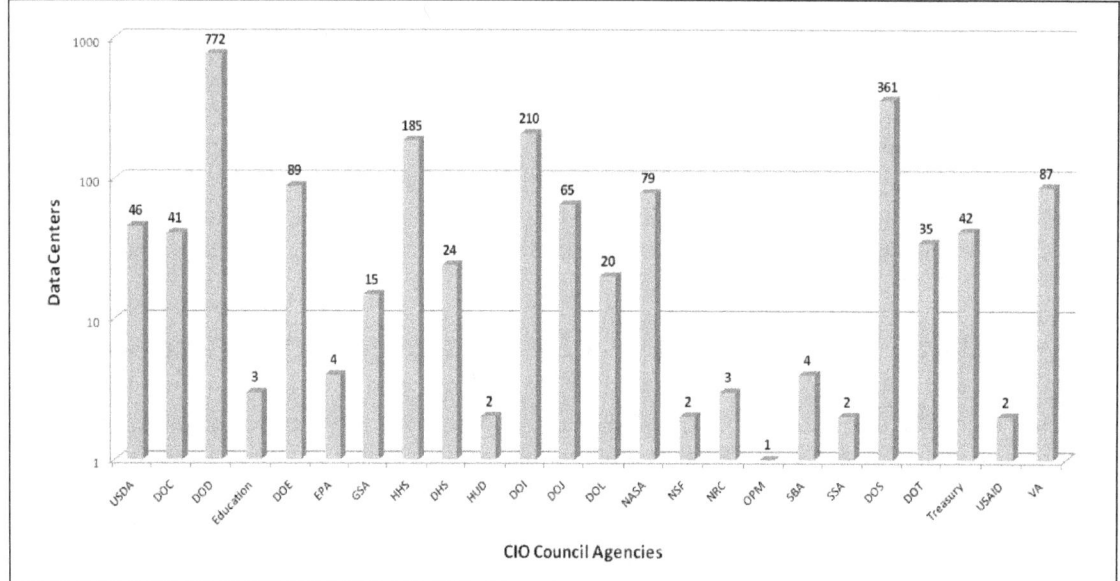

Source: Vivek Kundra and Richard Spires, "Update on the Federal Data Center Consolidation Initiative," Memorandum for Chief Information Officers, October 1, 2010.

Within the context of the current federal consolidation initiative, DOD's efforts are intended to address concerns about rising energy demands and costs of data centers, associated increases in carbon emissions, expanding real-estate footprints of data centers, and rising real-estate costs. According to DOD, it plans to reduce the number of its data centers by about 30% by 2013 (**Table 1**), and the number of servers by 25%. DOD intends to use savings generated from consolidation to pay the consolidation costs. It also plans to use cloud computing, where appropriate, as part of its consolidation and money-saving efforts.

Table 1. Current DOD Data Centers and Reductions Planned by FY2013

	Current	Planned
Air Force	137	117
Army	250	154
Navy	78	77
Combatant Commands	25	21
Other	282	163
Total	**772**	**532**

Source: Department of Defense.

Notes: Data for the "Other" category are tentative.

Further, also within DOD, the Defense Information Services Agency (DISA) has reportedly reduced its Defense Enterprise Computing Centers from 50 to 14 and is concentrating data centers on military bases as part of base realignment and closure. The Army began a major consolidation effort in 2006, although that project has faced obstacles, and the service has decided to use the DISA centers as part of its strategy. The Army capped data center growth in June 2010, concurrent with the government-wide announcement from the White House, and currently plans a 75% reduction, to 65 data centers by 2015. They did the same in January 2011, along with a planned 25% reduction in data centers, and a planned increase in server use and virtualization.

Status of DOD Data Center Consolidation

In its July 2011 report on the status of the FDCCI, the GAO reported that both DOD's current asset inventory (what the DOD currently has) and its consolidation plan were incomplete. DOD released its own report in November 2011[23] that provided an overview of DOD activities, but did not address the recommendations made by GAO.

Although no specific assessment of DOD has been conducted, GAO has published its findings regarding duplicative IT investments by the DOD and DOE and discusses the FDCCI within the context of overall IT reform.[24]

Issues for Congress

Achieving effective Congressional oversight of the FDCCI will require awareness of the program and an understanding of the management challenges and policy considerations involved with data center consolidation. Additionally, Congress may wish to examine the current "reach" of the FDCCI and consider whether expanding the initiative to include other agencies, as the GAO has recommended, is appropriate.

---

[23] 2011 Data Center Consolidation Plan and Progress Report, November 2011, DOD, http://dodcio.defense.gov/Portals/ 0/Documents/FDCCI-Final-2011.pdf. *"2011 DOD Report."*

[24] Departments of Defense and Energy Need to Address Potentially Duplicative Investments, GAO, February 2012, http://www.gao.gov/assets/590/588656.pdf.

FDCCI Awareness

Although this report discusses the DOD's implementation of the FDCCI, the initiative applies to 24 federal departments and agencies.

There is no single committee that has jurisdiction over the FDCCI; therefore, unlike many programs that are overseen by a single committee in each the Senate and the House, implementation of the FDCCI may require oversight by any number of committees with legislative jurisdiction. Although committees are experts on the departments and agencies they oversee, they may need additional expertise to understand and assess the impact of technologies such as data centers and cloud computing.

Awareness throughout Congress of the consolidation initiative, as well as the general management challenges and policy considerations issues outlined below, may also assist committees in achieving effective oversight and, from GAO's assessments, oversight is necessary. GAO has repeatedly stated that

> moving forward to consolidate obviously redundant or underutilized centers is warranted—and should result in immediate cost savings and increased efficiency ... the success of the initiative will be based, in large part, on continued efforts to oversee the development of complete inventories and comprehensive consolidation plans. Without either, there is an increased risk that departments and agencies will be ill-prepared to manage a transformation as significant as that which has been proposed by the Federal CIO. Such a lack of preparation could slow the consolidations and reduce expected savings and efficiencies.[25]

Data Center Consolidation Management Challenges and Policy Considerations

Any organization consolidating its data centers, whether in the private or public sector, will have up-front costs. Investing in those costs can provide many benefits, but challenges do exist and need to be closely monitored by managers and policymakers alike.

Up-Front Costs versus Ongoing Savings

Departments and agencies participating in the FDCCI will have some up-front costs, such as moving or replacing hardware and upgrading facilities, and the disposition of facility leases and equipment (leased or owned). While there appears to be a consensus that the ongoing operational savings can substantially outweigh such initial costs, that may not always be the case, and there is some evidence that such efforts may be difficult, complicated by factors such as incompatible hardware and a procurement process that may create barriers to consolidation.

Actual ongoing operational savings will depend on several factors. Policymakers may find it difficult to determine these savings in the absence of accurate and complete baseline measurements of energy and other costs. The FDCCI requires that plans include an explicit cost-benefit analysis. However, such an analysis requires either metering of data-center energy use or

---

[25] *GAO Report, Managing for Results,* pp. 54-55.

accurate estimates derived from modeling efforts. Neither source of information seems to be available for most federal data centers.

The focus of the effort is also important. For example, a consolidation project that focuses on hardware savings may result in much lower savings than one that also includes operations and other costs.

Maintaining Data Security

The reliance on cloud computing as an alternative to data centers could have a negative impact on data security if the consolidation process is not managed correctly. Consolidation will result in an increase in the number of users relying on any particular data center. Under some parts of the federal initiative, that will include other agencies. However, security was considered the biggest obstacle to such efforts by half of the respondents to a 2009 survey of federal agencies (more than four times higher than other factors such as cost). While improved security is cited as part of the rationale for the consolidation initiative, it is not clear how the security challenges it poses and the concerns expressed in the survey will be addressed. In the case of cloud computing, in contrast, the CIO Council responded to such concerns by establishing a specific security effort called the Federal Risk and Authorization Management Program (FedRAMP).[26] That program might also be relevant to the consolidation initiative.

Facilities Design and Energy Savings

The large overall percentage of data-center energy expended for cooling (see **Figure 1**) has focused increased attention on the role of facilities' design and operation. Specific criteria to increase the energy efficiency of data centers will be included in the new version of the LEED or similar industry rating system for green buildings. The Energy Star program has also developed an initiative to promote energy-efficient facilities design. A number of legislated mandates and executive branch policies continue to foster improved federal building energy efficiency and reduce federal energy use, with no exceptions made for data centers.

In its 2007 report, EPA had projected that national data-center energy use would double nearly twice between 2000 and 2011, and represent 100 billion kWh annually at a cost of $7.4 billion. A number of factors call EPA's estimates into question, including the lack of accurate metering by data centers and the aggregation of center electricity costs with their host facilities. Therefore, it was not possible to determine the likelihood that the estimate was either too high or too low. Even if the energy-use projection is accurate, the cost estimate might be low given increases in electricity rates.

---

[26] The Federal Risk and Authorization Management Program (FedRAMP) is a government-wide program that provides a standardized approach to security assessment, authorization, and continuous monitoring for cloud products and services. This approach uses a "do once, use many times" framework that will save cost, time, and staff required to conduct redundant agency security assessments. FedRAMP was established on December 8, 2011, via an official memorandum from the Federal Chief Information Officer to all agency CIOs. For additional information, see http://www.gsa.gov/portal/category/102371.

FDCCI Oversight by Congress

The appropriate Congressional committee may wish to monitor the progress of the department or agency under its jurisdiction. It may do this by holding hearings; requesting review of an agency's status through either the agency itself or a GAO study; or assessing the department or agency's progress and projected goals against the stated goals of the FDCCI.

Hearings

The OMB oversees the management of the FDCCI at the agency level. As such, it is the central point of information regarding the status of agency planning and implementation. More importantly, if OMB management practices are lacking in any way, the impact will be far reaching, potentially having a negative impact on the performance of all agencies as they implement their FDCCI plans. Consistent Congressional review of OMB's management practices could help detect and correct problems sooner than they might with that review. Committees may also wish to hold hearings to receive status reports directly from the CIO of the department or agency under their jurisdiction.

Review of Department and Agency FDCCI Plans and Assessments

As plans to consolidate data centers within the federal government are created and implemented, policymakers may want to monitor how departments and agencies are following the federal directives and responding to GAO assessments. Such monitoring can be achieved through assessments conducted internally by the department or agency itself or externally by GAO or the committee of jurisdiction.

Review of Internal Status Reports

Congress may monitor individual departments' and agencies' implementation of the FDCCI through regular reporting. For example, DOD released its own report in November 2011[27] that provided an overview of DOD activities, but did not address the recommendations made by GAO. Congress may want to provide more specific direction regarding the content of such reports, e.g., requiring a response to GAO findings in department and agency status reports.

Review of External Status Reports

Congress may also request that GAO conduct regular reviews of department and agency FDCCI progress. GAO reported comprehensively on the status of the overall progress of the FDCCI in its July 2011 report, but has not provided any department or agency-specific reports. Such reports might be able to be produced more quickly and released as they are completed, rather than in one report containing the status off all the departments and agencies. The committee of jurisdiction may also decide to conduct its own investigation.

---

[27] *2011 DOD Report.*

Expansion of the FDCCI

The GAO has also recommended that the FDCCI could be expanded to include other members of the Chief Information Officer Council, such as the Office of the Director of National Intelligence, and other independent executive branch agencies, such as the Securities and Exchange Commission and the Federal Communications Commission. Congress may wish to explore the feasibility, benefits, and drawbacks of that suggestion and make its own recommendations.

Appendix A. Related Laws

There are eight laws related to federal energy and data center management.

National Energy Conservation Policy Act[28]
P.L. 95-619
Consolidated Omnibus Budget Reconciliation Act of 1985[29]
P.L. 99-272

The 1978 National Energy Conservation Policy Act (NECPA, P.L. 95-619) initiated a program of retrofitting federal buildings to improve energy efficiency. It also required federal agencies, including DOD, to report annually on its progress in meeting energy consumption goals for facilities. The Consolidated Omnibus Budget Reconciliation Act of 1985 (also called the Deficit Reduction Act, P.L. 99-272) amended NECPA by authorizing energy savings contracts of up to 25 years. The 1992 Energy Policy Act (P.L. 102-486) further amended NECPA by adopting Energy Savings Performance Contracts (ESPCs) that offered federal agencies a novel means of making energy efficiency improvements to aging buildings and facilities (see discussion below).

Federal Energy Management Improvement Act of 1988[30]
P.L. 100-615

The Federal Energy Management Improvement Act of 1988 (P.L. 100-615) amended NECPA by requiring each agency to achieve a 10% reduction in energy consumption in federal buildings by FY1995 when measured against an FY1985 baseline in terms of British thermal units per gross square foot of building area. By FY2005, DOD reported a 28.3% reduction in energy consumption compared to the FY1985 baseline. Federal agencies report their energy consumption annually to Congress through FEMP.

Energy Policy Act of 1992[31]
P.L. 102-486

Authorized energy savings performance contracts of up to 25 years.

Energy Policy Act of 2005[32]
P.L. 109-58

Section 103 of EPACT (Energy Use Measurement and Accountability) amended Section 543 of NECPA by mandating advanced meters in federal buildings by October 1, 2012, to assist in reducing electricity use. Advanced meters have the capability to measure and record interval data (at least hourly for electricity), and to communicate the data to a remote location in a format that can be easily integrated into an advanced metering system. Section 103 requires at least daily data

---

[28] Online at http://www1.eere.energy.gov/femp/regulations/necpa html and http://uscode house.gov/download/pls/ 42C91.txt.

[29] A summary of this law is online at http://goo.gl/a6p9j.

[30] A summary of this law is online at http://goo.gl/kiZKF.

[31] Online at http://www1.eere.energy.gov/femp/regulations/epact1992 html.

[32] Online at http://www1.eere.energy.gov/femp/regulations/epact2005 html.

collection capability. Advanced metering offers the means to measure, verify, and optimize performance, including diagnosing equipment and systems operations, and to thereby promote energy use awareness for building managers and occupants. However, the EPACT requirement applies to entire buildings, not data centers within those buildings. Section 922 established a DOE research and development program to improve energy efficiency of data centers and other high energy-density facilities. Also, Section 104 established the requirement that federal agencies purchase Energy Star or FEMP-designate products discussed in the section on "Data-Center Power Consumption."

To Study and Promote the Use of Energy Efficient Computer Servers in the United States[33]
P.L. 109-431

Required the Administrator of the Environmental Protection Agency, through the Energy Star program, to study and report on the rapid growth and energy consumption of computer data centers by the federal government and private enterprise. The EPA responded with Report to Congress on Server and Data Center Energy Efficiency (August 2, 2007).

Energy Independence and Security Act of 2007[34]
P.L. 110-140

Section 431 (Energy Reduction Goals for Federal Buildings) amended the National Energy Conservation Policy Act (NECPA) by mandating a 30% energy reduction in federal buildings by 2015 relative to a 2005 baseline. Section 432 (Management of Energy and Water Efficiency in Federal Buildings) required DOE to issue guidelines and criteria that each federal agency will follow for designating "covered facilities," assigning energy managers, and implementing comprehensive energy and water evaluations. For the purpose of energy and water evaluations, covered facilities constitute at least 75% of facility energy use at each facility. Section 434 (Management of Federal Building Efficiency) required that federal agencies ensure the energy life-cycle cost effectiveness of major equipment replacements (such as heating and cooling systems) and renovations or expansion of existing space. Section 453 (Energy Efficiency for Data Center Buildings) established a joint DOE-EPA national information program on data-center energy efficiency.

Intelligence Authorization Act for FY2010[35]
P.L. 111-259

Sec. 414 (Plan to Implement Recommendations of the Data Center Energy Efficiency Reports) directed the National Intelligence Director to develop a plan to implement the recommendations of the study completed under P.L. 109-431.

---

[33] Online at http://www.gpo.gov/fdsys/pkg/PLAW-109publ431/pdf/PLAW-109publ431.pdf.

[34] Online at http://www1.eere.energy.gov/femp/regulations/eisa html.

[35] Online at http://www.gpo.gov/fdsys/pkg/PLAW-111publ259/pdf/PLAW-111publ259.pdf.

Appendix B. Related Executive Orders

There are three Executive Orders related to energy management.

Energy Efficient Standby Power Devices
Executive Order 13221, signed by President Bush on August 2, 2001

Requires federal agencies to purchase products that use no more than one watt in standby power consuming mode when purchasing commercially available, off-the-shelf products that use external standby power devices or that contain an internal standby power function.

If such products are not available, agencies must purchase products with the lowest standby power wattage while in their standby power consuming mode.

Requires agencies to adhere to this Order when life-cycle cost-effective and practicable, and where the relevant product's utility and performance are not compromised as a result.

Requires, beginning December 31, 2001, and on an annual basis thereafter, the Department of Energy, in consultation with the Department of Defense and the General Services Administration, to compile a preliminary list of products to be subject to these requirements.

Requires that the Department of Energy finalize the list and remove products deemed inappropriate for listing.

Strengthening Federal Environmental, Energy, and Transportation Management[36]
Executive Order 13423, signed by President Bush, January 24, 2007

Instructs federal agencies to conduct their environmental, transportation, and energy-related activities under the law in support of their respective missions in an environmentally, economically, and fiscally sound, integrated, continuously improving, efficient, and sustainable manner.

The Order sets goals in the area of electronics stewardship, among others.

Federal Leadership In Environmental, Energy and Economic Performance[37]
Executive Order 13514, signed by President Obama Oct 5, 2009

Requires that federal agencies take further steps to ensure that their IT purchases are energy efficient or otherwise environmentally friendly.

Specifically requires federal agencies to promote electronics stewardship, in particular by implementing best management practices for energy-efficient management of servers and federal data centers.

---

[36] Online at http://www.epa.gov/oaintrnt/practices/eo13423 htm.

[37] Online at http://www.epa.gov/oaintrnt/practices/eo13514 htm.

For further background information on EO 13514, see CRS Report R40974, *Executive Order 13514: Sustainability and Greenhouse Gas Emissions Reduction* , by Richard J. Campbell and Anthony Andrews.

Author Contact Information

Patricia Moloney Figliola, Coordinator
Specialist in Internet and Telecommunications
Policy
pfigliola@crs.loc.gov, 7-2508

Anthony Andrews
Specialist in Energy and Defense Policy
aandrews@crs.loc.gov, 7-6843

Eric A. Fischer
Senior Specialist in Science and Technology
efischer@crs.loc.gov, 7-7071